The Square Book Of Animals

THE SQUARE BOOK OF ANIMALS
By William Nicholson.

RHYMES BY ARTHUR WAUGH.

Published by R.H.Russell. New York. 1900.

AN EXPLANATION

Friend, seek not here (to feed the mind)
    Zoology's recondite feasts:
Here you will find but common, kind,
    And unsophisticated beasts!

Yet fresh the life of farm and grange
    As that which o'er the ocean roams;
Take for a change a narrower range—
    An English book for English homes!

THE BRITISH BULL-DOG

You swing the gate; and there he stands to greet you,
  With growl or grin, as you are strange or known:
According to your merits will he treat you—
  An Englishman who loves and guards his own.

THE UN-COMMON CAT

Nine lives they give the common cat?
There's a rare one livelier yet than that!
A cat that swings nine separate tails!
And, when it's let out of the bag, it rails
With so knotty a tongue that the culprit quails!

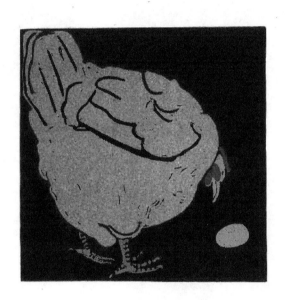

THE FRIENDLY HEN

Some birds lay eggs in towering trees,
And some in fens conceal them;
The hen seeks friendlier haunts than these,
Where every child can steal them.

THE LEARNED PIG

The farm's philosophy, our eyes assure us,
    Is simpler than in Aristotle's day:
The youngest pigling follows Epicurus,
    And Bacon's Essays take the primrose way.

THE BEAUTIFUL SWAN

All day she rules the pond from edge to edge,
Exerting Beauty's easy privilege;
Her world a mirror spread in each direction,
Where she reflects upon her own reflection.

THE VERY TAME LAMB

All men, said the poet, are struck at a mint,
    And some coins ring flat that the coiners embellish;
But the lamb is so tame he will pardon the hint—
    He'd be best with a little mint-*sauce* for a relish!

THE TOILSOME GOAT

"You're a lively kid!" is the schoolboy jest;
    But the kid is driven to work one day,
And the hours of harness know little rest
    For the stiff goat-carriage round the bay.

THE LUCKY DUCK

There was a Drake, my Duck, at Plymouth Hoe
    Played bowls, with Spain's Armada clear of Dover!
A gamesome spirit! But to him we owe
The peace your farm and all our homesteads know:
For, ere the Spaniard reached our wickets, lo!
    Drake bowled him over!

COCK O' THE NORTH

Cock o' the North! The dawn is young,
    Grey-glimmering the pane;
Yet you, with your discordant tongue,
    Have woken me again!
Good beasts are silent in their pens.
Hush! Leave the boasting to the hens!

THE SIMPLE SHEEP

The sheep's like the man in the street.
She will follow, and blunder, and bleat,
   In pursuit of her fate
   At the slaughter-house gate,
And she learns it too late to retreat.

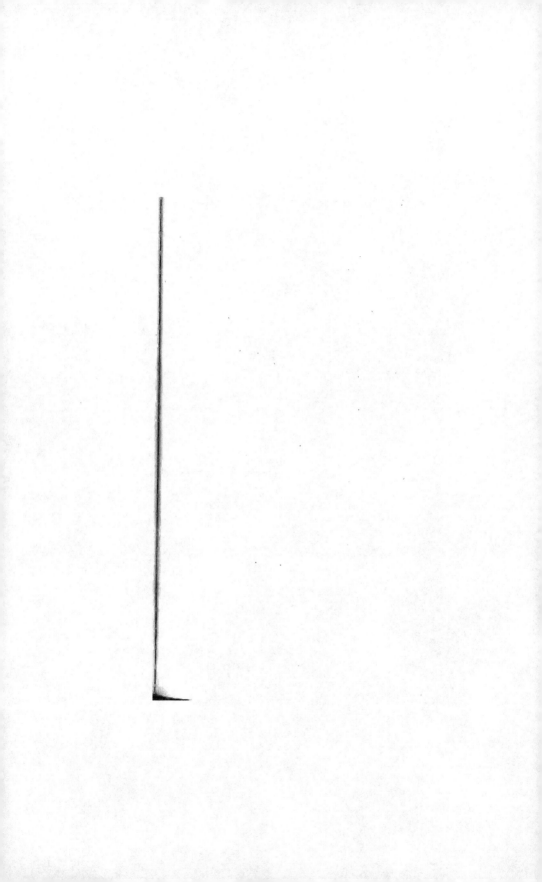

THE SERVILE COW

When the cow's in the farmyard, her sense
Of servility's simply immense;
   But you meet her again
   In the highway or lane,
And she tosses you over the fence.

THE GROWING COLT

Rough, shaggy colt: the world is all before you:
    Blithe be your life, secure of oats and hay;
A little crowd of people to adore you,
    And some green resting-place at shut of day!

The sun is low behind the grey-green trees.

And all the farm grows quiet by degrees.

Among their many lessons this is best:

The animals know when and how to rest!

                                                  A. W.

CPSIA information can be obtained
at www.ICGtesting.com
Printed in the USA
LVHW081337230919
631970LV00005B/83/P

9 781375 826297